Everyday Heroes

Learning from the Careers of Successful Black Professionals

Everyday Heroes

Learning from the Careers of Successful Black Professionals

Frances Mensah Williams

SKN Publishing

Published by SKN Publishing 2011

Reprinted 2012

A division of Interims for Development Ltd.

Kingsbury House, 468 Church Lane, London NW9 8UA

A CIP catalogue record for this book is available from the British Library

ISBN 978-0-9569175-0-8

Prepared and printed by

York Publishing Services
64 Hallfield Road
Layerthorpe
York YO31 7ZQ

www.yps-publishing.co.uk

For my brother Thomas

(1959-2007)

My hero, today and everyday

Reviews of Everyday Heroes

Everyday Heroes reminds us that there are many paths to success. The inspiring message from the contributors is the same – work hard and learn from everyone and everything around you. A fascinating and informative collection of interviews which will inspire younger and older readers alike.

ELSIE OWUSU OBE RIBA
PRINCIPAL, ELSIE OWUSU ARCHITECTS LTD

This is not the first book aimed at raising the aspirations of African/ Caribbean children, but where it differs from most is that it takes "success" away from the realms of celebrity, and grounds it in the reality of those unsung heroes all around you. So let's stop expecting Trevor Macdonald, Diane Abbott or Rio Ferdinand or Lewis Hamilton to inspire our children, and point out some everyday heroes closer to home, because in my experience, they usually bring more sustainable results.

HENRY BONSU
JOURNALIST & BROADCASTER,
COLOURFUL RADIO, VOX AFRICA

Contents

Everyday heroes are people from our communities who have achieved success in their own areas of activity and who inspire us to do better.

Acknowledgements

"At times our own light goes out and is rekindled by a spark from another person. Each of us has cause to think with deep gratitude of those who have lighted the flame within us."

Albert Schweitzer

I once heard that real success is about creating opportunities for other people. So with *Everyday Heroes* I wanted to capture the stories of people who have created opportunities for others, whether or not they knew it.

Because even those who don't see themselves as role models are unwittingly creating opportunities for others just by doing what they do, and by doing it with integrity and to the best of their ability.

My love and thanks to my daughter Seena who first sparked the idea of *Everyday Heroes* as we debated the lessons of the American civil rights era and wondered how to turn the spotlight onto today's role models. To Elvina, Kwadua, Onyekachi, Simi and Lande, who listened patiently to me as I developed the concept, thank you for your time, your feedback and all your insights and suggestions. My thanks also go to my wonderful father for his proofreading skills and unfailing support and to Oba, Henry and Elsie for your kind comments about the book. Each of you merits a book to yourself for the inspiration that you provide to others.

My thanks to Mike Higgins for your wonderful input into the careers exercises and to Caite for your taster session on IP. To Helen, thank you for your generous and invaluable pointers, for your positive spirit and for keeping me laughing!

To my husband, Nana, thank you for your encouragement and support and for the home-cooked meals while I was glued to the computer. And thanks to my daughter, Khaya, without whose constant hugs and cuddles this book would have been finished so much sooner – but with not nearly as much love.

To the amazing team at YPS who brought this book to life, my deep appreciation for your patience and professionalism.

Last, but certainly not least, my thanks and gratitude go to all of the fascinating black professionals who agreed to be part of *Everyday Heroes* and to share their experiences.

I know for sure that your stories and your advice will be the spark that ignites and rekindles the light for many.

Foreword

As I read **Everyday Heroes**, it reminded me of something once said by Malcolm Forbes: "Education's purpose is to replace an empty mind with an open one". This for me encapsulates the power in reading about ordinary people who have achieved extraordinary things.

There are so few similar books in this neglected market and, with its unique approach, **Everyday Heroes** reminds us that those who walk in the tracks of others leave no footprints of their own.

However, the real success of this book lies not just in the stories it tells, but in how it does the telling. It not only challenges us to leave our own individual tracks, but explains how we can identify and develop our own unique footprints to create those tracks. It does this by speaking to the everyday heroes of tomorrow in a direct and practical style which demystifies the career quagmire and allows for a much better understanding of who they are and what they can become with hard work and persistence.

Therefore, "if you can imagine it, you can create it. If you can dream it, you can become it." Look no further than yourselves for the next generation of **Everyday Heroes**.

Professor Oba Nsugbe QC, SAN.

What Makes a Hero?

Heroes can come in all shapes and sizes but what makes them heroic is their ability to move us; to make us see how we too can be bigger and better, and can aim higher and achieve more than, perhaps, we thought we could.

For the most part, we tend to think of heroes as people who are quite distant from us. Famous singers, actors, television stars – people we will probably never meet but whose lives make us believe that we can be or do anything.

These distant heroes can be inspirational but sometimes, when their lives seem so very different from ours, it can also be quite hard to imagine how we can reach their level of success.

When we put too much emphasis on distant heroes, it can also make us forget that we are surrounded by heroes in our everyday lives; heroes we don't always see or appreciate because we don't know their stories. Because they look like us, we don't ask too many questions about what they do and sometimes, when we do ask, their jobs and careers often sound quite complicated and hard to understand.

And because these people are not famous and we don't know what they do or what they had to go through to be able to do it, we don't realise that we have heroes right in front of us, every day.

Growing up in a society where we look different from most of the people around us can be difficult. People can pick on us because we have different colour skin, because we dress differently or even because we have a different accent. Instead of being proud of our beautiful skins and remembering that an accent means that we are clever enough to speak more than one language, we can instead sometimes feel sad and isolated from others.

I wrote *Everyday Heroes* because I think it's time to tell the stories of the heroes who are right here next to us and who look and sound like us. I believe that by telling you about the lives of successful people who are around us every day and by sharing their advice, it will give you a chance to learn from them and to have a better understanding of what it takes to be a success at whatever you choose to do.

Everyday Heroes is also designed to help you find your own everyday heroes and to think about what their lessons mean for your future. At the end of the book, you are asked to think about what you've learned from these everyday heroes and to think about a career that would suit you and what you need to do to reach your goals. Start taking action today for your future career and see how you can become an everyday hero of tomorrow.

Are you ready to be inspired?

Jacqueline Musiitwa

Lawyer & Managing Partner

Jacqueline Musiitwa founded and acts as Managing Partner of Hoja Law Group, a boutique New York law firm which represents government ministries, businesses and non-profits in areas of political, corporate and intellectual property law.

Hoja Law Group also specializes in assisting investors doing business in and/or investing in Africa. She is spending the next year in Rwanda as an advisor to the Minister of Justice on legal matters related to trade and investment. Jacqueline was at Pillsbury Winthrop Shaw Pittman LLP, where she practiced in the area of corporate law and also clerked for Denton Wilde Sapte's Zambia affiliate office, Corpus Legal Practitioners.

Jacqueline is the founder of Transitional Trade, a non-profit whose mission it is to promote social trade, investment and entrepreneurship in post-conflict countries and transitional communities.

She has participated in the rebranding of several countries, advising African companies as well as mentoring many African entrepreneurs.

Additionally, Jacqueline is a Senior Associate with the African European Affairs Consulting group which advises clients on matters including but not limited to corporate strategy, risk management and corporate governance.

Jacqueline has been an Adjunct Professor of International Law at Central Michigan University and of Sociopolitics and Economics of Africa at Drexel University.

I was educated at...

... Davidson College (BA in Political Science and International Studies), the Australian National University (Post Graduate Diploma in Legal Practice), and the University of Melbourne (Juris Doctor).

My first job was...

... at a global law firm called Pillsbury Winthrop Shaw Pittman, LLP.

What I do now is...

... run a boutique law firm called Hoja Law Group that specializes in advising clients with an interest in Africa. Among other things, we advise on contracts between African businesses contracting with American businesses, as well as investors investing in Africa. I am spending a year in Rwanda, advising the Minister of Justice on legal matters related to trade and investment.

What I learned along the way is...

... many things in life. A few of my greatest lessons have been:

- Be patient, things happen in their own time and shape themselves in the way the Universe wants them to be.

- Attitude puts you a step beyond the rest. Your attitude determines how far you go in life.

- Work hard in all you do, but also have fun doing whatever it is you do. It makes the task at hand much more effortless.

My greatest influence has been...

... female leaders generally, starting with my mother who has been my cheerleader from day one and who has emphasized the importance of leading a life based on solid morals and commitment to improving the lives of others. I am inspired by Ellen Sirleaf Johnson (President of Liberia), Aloysie Cyanzaire (Chief Justice of the Supreme Court, Rwanda), Hillary Clinton (Secretary of State, USA) and many more because they provide a great precedent for the achievements women can make.

The best advice I ever received was.....

… stay true to yourself.

My top tips for succeeding in my career are.....

• Always be curious. That way you are always learning and coming up with creative solutions to problems.

• Study hard, but don't forget that learning is not limited to books. Expose yourself to different types of people, different types of jobs/work environments and different situations.

• Keep up to date with the news. A lot of things in the area of law are affected by current affairs, so it is not only essential to know the letter of the law, it is important to understand the policy implications and the wider reach of the law.

Eugene Skeef

Composer & Poet

Eugene Skeef FRSA is a South African percussionist, composer, poet, educationalist and animator and has lived in London since 1980. He also works in conflict resolution, acts as a consultant on cultural development, teaches creative leadership and is a broadcaster. In 2003 he founded Umoya Creations, a charity set up to facilitate this international work.

As a young activist he co-led a nationwide literacy campaign teaching in schools, colleges and communities across apartheid South Africa. As well as being at the forefront of the contemporary music scene and collaborating with innovative artists, he has also been instrumental in developing the education programmes of some of the major classical orchestras in the United Kingdom.

Eugene is a Fellow of the Royal Society of Arts and sits on the board of directors of the London Philharmonic Orchestra. He is on the advisory committee of Sound Junction, the Associated Board of the Royal Schools of Music's award-winning interactive multimedia educational project. In September 2004 he was appointed musician in residence of the Purcell School of Music. In March 2005 Eugene performed with his Abantu Ensemble at Buckingham Palace and was presented to the Queen as part of the historic Music Day to celebrate the diversity of culture in Britain.

In 2008, Eugene and Richard Bissill's *Excite!* – an orchestral commission by the LPO – premiered at the Royal Festival Hall at Southbank Centre, London. Eugene is the Artistic Director of Quartet of Peace, an international project initiated by Brian Lisus, the South African luthier who has made a quartet of string instruments in honour of South Africa's 4 Nobel peace laureates: Dr. Albert Luthuli, Nelson Mandela, Archbishop Desmond Tutu and FW de Klerk. Quartet of Peace uses music to bring about peaceful resolutions to conflict and poverty, with a special focus on young people.

I was educated at...

... a primary school in South Africa called St. Philomena's. It was a school far from my home and which was chosen by my mother as one she believed would provide her children with what she considered a good foundation to do well in the world of the white people. My secondary schooling was at Umbilo High School, where my political consciousness reached a peak of awareness. However, the education I received through my mother's magnanimity towards others, especially those more disadvantaged than herself, has to count as being the most important and sustainable in my life.

My first job was...

... working for a company called Soil & Rocks Mechanics Laboratory in Durban, South Africa, as a lab technician. I enjoyed the job because of the friendships I created – and our lunch hours playing football against the backdrop of the Indian Ocean.

What I do now is...

... create music. I live to make music and music is my living. Primarily, I am a musician and a composer. I perform occasionally for specific one-off events. I write music for choirs, orchestras, film and theatre. I run motivational, creative workshops for corporations (team-building); for communities (towards a performance, festival or for fun); for orchestras (to enhance musicianship and group dynamics); for nurseries and schools and for specialist schools of music. I compose and run music workshops for children and my work also entails travelling the world using my music as a healing tool and to resolve conflict in areas where young people, in particular, are damaged by war and religious and racial intolerance. I get invited to conferences and events to speak about my work and tell stories to inspire, guide, and, crucially, get people to think outside of the box. I give guidance on issues within cultural development and education through various boards and committees I sit on. Importantly, I am valued for not being afraid to challenge the status quo in order to enhance music appreciation, improve teaching, learning and performance. I judge competitions like Choir of the Year, a UK-wide challenge held every other year. I have presented specialist shows for BBC Radio 4 and sat on discussion and music panels for BBC Radio 3.

What I learned along the way is…

… that I am never bigger than anything or anyone around me; that I'm a small particle in the complex picture of life. My humility was taught to me first and foremost by my mother. She taught me never to prejudge and to be accepting of everyone I come into contact with. She encouraged me to enjoy a peaceful way of living in harmony with others; this is my biggest lesson and I continue to enact that in the way I live

My greatest influence has been…

… my mother, because she was the embodiment of love and from an early age instilled in me the need to be loving towards others. Before I express anger, I am quick to remember my mother who never scolded us in my whole life and I've developed techniques of using other and more fun ways of resolving conflicts.

The best advice I ever received was…..

… to give people the benefit of the doubt. More specifically, if I run into a situation where something upsets me; before I react, I always try to first take a breath, stop and consider.

My top tips for succeeding in my career are….

- Follow your instinct – it is not always that the world around us reflects our deepest insights and feelings about who we wish to be. Listening to your inner voice is a very good place to start. Find the determination to match what you "hear" with a personal vision of how you can make a meaningful difference or impact on the outside world.

- Find your icon – look for someone who has made a success of the career you are attracted to, and ask them for their advice. Interview the person in such a way as to make them feel good about sharing the story of their success in their chosen career.

- Sense of play – try to retain your natural sense of play. Most of us lose this vital natural disposition when we become adults, wrongly thinking that play is good only for children. The opposite is true. When we play, we are relaxed. Relaxation is the key to self-confidence and the inspiration of confidence in those with whom we interact. When you inspire confidence in others, they become more welcoming towards you and your ideas. Relaxation will also enhance your ability to achieve difficult tasks.

Mame Gyang

Project Manager

Mame Gyang is the Special Projects Manager responsible for managing the support and delivery of critical projects for Enfield Council's Health & Adult Social Care Services.

A Prince 2 qualified Project Manager, Mame's role includes preparing Project Initiation Documents, setting up issue/risk logs, identifying key milestones and establishing and supporting the project teams. Tasked with ensuring that deadlines are met and objectives achieved, she also prepares briefings and presentations for Cabinet and Senior Management of the Council.

Born in Ghana, Mame studied Estate Management at the Kwame Nkrumah University of Science and Technology before moving to the UK to work in property management.

Following a career change into the retail sector where she took on responsibility for managing a Customer Care Desk, Mame moved to Brent Council in 1996 to manage a team of ten staff delivering a front line service for Brent's customers.

In her role today at Enfield Council, which she joined in January 2003, Mame also holds responsibility for Equalities and co-ordinates and collates equalities returns, monitoring information which supports Health & Adult Social Care staff to implement all requirements on the six equality strands and to develop services in accordance with legislation.

The busy mother of two is an avid reader and film buff who enjoys writing poetry, listening to music and cooking for family and friends.

I was educated at…

… the University of Science & Technology, Kumasi, Ghana, where I studied Estate Management.

My first job was…..

… as an Estate Manager.

What I do now is….

… Special Projects Manager, Health and Adult Social Care for Enfield Council in London, where I am responsible for project management to support the delivery of the Division's priority and other critical projects.

What I learned along the way is…

… life is short; enjoy it.

My greatest influence has been…..

… my mother, because she was a strong, practical woman and was a role model for a working mother like me. She worked full-time and still managed to bring up four children who have gone on to have successful careers.

The best advice I ever received is…..

… always make sure that whatever you do, you do to the best of your ability and are proud to put your name to it.

My top tips for succeeding in my career are…..

*   You will need to have the ability to plan and organise.

*   Be a 'completer finisher'; make sure you finish everything you start.

- Be a great team player.

- You must learn to manage conflict and disagreements.

- You must become effective at finding solutions.

- You will need to develop the ability to deal with any challenges.

Danny John-Jules

Actor & Entertainer

Danny John-Jules trained at the Omnibus Theatre Company and Anna Scher Children's Theatre. His theatre credits include *Night and Day*, the UK premiere of *Carmen Jones*, *Destry Rides Again* at the Donmar Warehouse and *Labelled with Love* at the Albany Empire.

In the West End, Danny has appeared in *Barnum* at the London Palladium, *CATS* and *TIME*. He created the role of 'Rocky 1' in *Starlight Express* at the Apollo, Victoria, and was 'Dink' in the first West End production of *Carmen Jones* at the Old Vic Theatre for director Simon Callow and musical director Henry Lewis.

In 1994, he played 'Avery' in August Wilson's *The Piano Lesson* (directed by Paulette Randall) and 'Mac', the Playboy's father, in *The Playboy of the West Indies*, before going on to appear in *The Rover* at Jacob Street Film Studios, directed by Jules Wright for the Women's Playhouse Trust – the production was also filmed by BBC Television.

In 1995, Danny created the role of 'Neal' in *Lonely Hearts*, a new musical by Trisha Ward, at the Oxford Fire Station, before going on to play 'Robert Sideway' in *Our Country's Good* at Theatre Clwyd. Danny recently played "Jimi Hendrix" in a production called *The Devil's Interval* – which marks the year in which Jimi Hendrix would have been 60 – at The Handel Museum in London.

His film credits include *Seven Green Bottles, Scum, The Great Muppet Caper, Ragtime* and Hanif Kureishi's *London Kills Me* for Working Title Films, *Lock Stock and Two Smoking Barrels, Sleep* and *Blade 2* as "Assad" with Wesley Snipes and directed by Guillermo del Toro.

Danny's radio credits include *A City Called Glory*, the life story of Sam Cooke, for producer Andy Jordan at BBC Radio and *Can't Catch Me* for producer Nandita Ghose for BBC Radio 4.

I was educated at…

… Rutherford Comprehensive on the Edgware Road in London.

My first job was…

… a building site labourer.

What I do now is…

… I am an actor and entertainer.

What I learned along the way is…

… you have to be twice as good as you think you are.

My greatest influence has been…

… family…and Charles Augins (American actor, dancer and choreographer)

The best advice I ever received was…

… (American Accent) "You Black, you always gonna be Black, and as long as you live, racism gon' be there, dig?"

My top tips for succeeding in my career are…

•   Watch the good actors, which usually means going back in time.

•   Remember that rejection will always be lurking in the shadows.

•   You will have to twice as good as your European counterparts.

•   Know the business you are entering; books, videos, movies – 'you've got to be in it to win it!'

Simi Belo

Inventor & Entrepreneur

Described by PR Week as "having an obvious aptitude for PR", Simi Belo has over fourteen years experience in Public Relations (PR) and Marketing and ran her own PR consultancy Guru PR Ltd. Before that, Simi was as an associate director at Text 100 – the international IT PR consultancy renowned for handling the launch of Microsoft. For three years before joining Text 100, Simi headed up the UK PR department of Electronic Arts (EA), famous for top-selling video games.

A graduate from King's College, University of London, Simi also has a PRCA Post-graduate Diploma in International Public Relations, and a CIM Post-Graduate Diploma in Marketing. Simi is an active member of many networks and helps a variety of charities and trusts, encouraging entrepreneurialism amongst the youth and advising start-up companies.

For many years, Simi has been simply desperate to improve the products available for women and she has had many ideas. In 2003, she finally developed one of her favourite ideas: a unique type of hair extensions. Four months later, in January 2004, reputable UK shops and salons, including Selfridges, were selling her revolutionary 'NewHair™' (now Simiweave™) and by October 2004, it was available in the US and Canada under exclusive license.

Heralded as 'a new invention set to take the hairdressing world by storm' by industry-leading magazine Black Beauty & Hair, Simiweave™ has been an overnight success amongst customers, hair and beauty experts, the media, celebrities and retailers alike. It has won major awards including 'European Business 2004' from the European Federation of Black Women Business Owners, while Simi was a finalist for the 'Women in Business' Start-ups 2005 award and the 'International Business Woman of the Year' 2005 award.

I was educated at…

… primary school in Lagos, Nigeria; secondary and University were at King's College, University of London, followed by a Masters degree in the UK.

My first job was…

… Regional Organiser for LEPRA, the charity for the relief of leprosy. It was an extremely challenging fund raising, marketing and events management role. I used to make presentations in assemblies at schools to inform the pupils that leprosy still existed, and every penny counted. And I had to organise street collections too – I'm still an expert at shaking a collection tin!

What I do now is…

… run an inventions company. We've launched one invention so far, the award-winning Simiweave® – a new type of wig/hair extensions designed specifically for Black women. My role is inventing, new business development and marketing.

What I learned along the way is…

… 'Make whatever you want happen; after all, the only regrets you should have in life are things that you've not done, not things that you've done.' 'You can't make an omelette without breaking eggs.' 'Life is what happens whilst you are too busy planning or dreaming.' 'Don't ask, don't get.' And here are two I made up myself: 'Rules made by man were made to be broken by woman', and 'If it is important to you, leave your pride at the door.'

My greatest influence has been…….

… my parents for their guidance, determination and capacity for hard work and my ex-boss, Al King, for teaching me the importance of strategy.

The best advice I ever received is...

... 'Sometimes you win, sometimes you learn.' If you approach life like that, then the concept of failure will be alien to you. And without the fear of failure, the sky's the limit!

My top tips for succeeding in my career are...

- Be honest with yourself; know your interests and limitations or take the time to find out as soon as possible. You may not know what you want to do, but you must know what you don't want to do, or do not have the interest, desire or inclination for.

- In life, sometimes you win and sometimes you learn. So don't panic if your first career move or choice is not successful; every experience is valuable.

Allan Kamau

Publisher

Allan Kamau is the Associate Publisher of *This is Africa,* a quarterly published by the Financial Times Ltd, one of the world's leading business news organisations. Prior to this, Allan worked as Editor of Africa Investor magazine based in London, reporting on issues affecting Africa's trade and investment environment.

A graduate of the University of Nairobi, Allan subsequently earned an MBA from the United States International University. He joined Exxon Mobil Corporation in Kenya as a Public Affairs Advisor, relocating to the Paris office in 1999 as a Marketing Support Manager.

In 2000, Allan returned to Kenya as Marketing Manager for Nation Media Group, the leading East African newspaper publisher, TV, and radio broadcasting group, where he developed the ground breaking TV series "Business Minds", profiling top East Africa businesses, and was also lead presenter on Nation's TV's evening news.

In 2002, Allan moved to London to join LIMRA, a market intelligence provider specialising in the financial services sector, as Head of Marketing and Public Relations, for two years. For the next five years, as Managing Director of Africa Investor Ltd., Allan managed one of Africa's most respected publishing, research, and advisory firms.

Responsible for a team of twenty in the UK, South Africa, Nigeria, and Tanzania, he provided leadership for pan-African clients, advising on African economic issues, investment and media.

Allan is a frequent media commentator on business in Africa and serves on the advisory board of Junior Achievement in Africa.

I was educated at…

… St Mary's School, Nairobi, Kenya and the University of Nairobi.

My first job was…

… writing jingles for McCann Erickson advertising agency.

What I do now is…

… I am the Associate Publisher for This is Africa, Financial Times Ltd.

What I learned along the way is…

… find out what you are good at and give it your all.

My greatest influence has been…

… my family and friends.

The best advice I ever received was…

… don't compare yourself with others, just focus on doing your best.

My top tips for succeeding in my career are…

- Believe you can: believe that you are the best and that you are capable of achieving great things.

- Stick at it until you win: make a plan and be prepared to do the work to become a success.

- Be the best at your craft: invest in improving what you do and acquiring the skills to be the best.

Annmarie Dixon-Barrow OBE

Headhunter

Annmarie Dixon Barrow OBE has over twenty years of experience at all levels across public, private and voluntary sectors.

She has been responsible for developing programmes to generate employment opportunities for minority groups and renewing focus and reinvigorating activities within existing local, regional and national networks.

Annmarie has been instrumental in establishing new networks and coalitions to develop, implement and extend programmes and provides policy briefings to senior and board-level management for private and public sectors, NGOs and within local and central government

Annmarie is currently the Managing Director of annmarie consulting, offering a full range of tailored services on diversity and executive search. She is also Managing Director of The Black Excellence Network, that offers excellent opportunities to develop and deepen connections.

She has held board-level positions for the Open University, New Islington and Hackney Housing Association, Camden ITEC, the London Academy of Music and Dramatic Art (LAMDA) and the League of Mercy. A senior advisor to some of the world's largest companies, she is also a member of the Talent and Enterprise Advisory Group at the Department for Children, Schools and Families, Advisor to Time Warner Group and judge for The Power List.

I was educated at…

… City of Leeds High School.

My first job was…

… selling cool hippy clothes in a boutique in Leeds called Boodle-Am.

What I do now is…

… provide headhunting services – helping companies to find executives.

What I learned along the way is…

… deliver. You are only as good as the last piece of work you have delivered, so you have to put 100% into everything that you do and always do your best.

My greatest influence has been…

… my mother, because she came to England from Jamaica and brought up three children as a single mother after my father died. She managed to carve out a career and look after us and she really gave of herself to other people wherever she went. When she died, her funeral service was packed because so many people, from shopkeepers to politicians, turned up. My mother was very supportive of me and even when I didn't go to university as she wanted, she still supported everything that I chose to do.

The best advice I ever received is…

… don't forget where you have come from and bring other people with you.

My top tips for succeeding in my career are...

- Remember that headhunting can be a great career and is open to everybody. You don't need a university degree and headhunters come from all kinds of backgrounds.

- Headhunting is different to being a recruiter where you find staff for a company and get paid only when you find someone that they decide to hire. Headhunters have to develop a wide network of contacts and be able to build long-term relationships. They have to invest time and effort to know their clients and the candidates they offer to their clients' businesses. A good headhunter is a trusted adviser who also knows how to keep information confidential.

- To be a successful headhunter you have to be self-motivated because no-one else is there to do your job for you. You have to be able to be independent because you will effectively be running your own show.

- It's important to enjoy talking to people and listening to what they say, whether they are your clients or the candidates that you want to place in a job. Communication is really important because it's not about you, but about understanding what your client needs for their business and what a candidate needs in a job role.

- Treat people well. The candidate of today is your client of tomorrow and you have to think long-term, not just about today.

Tutu Agyare

Investment Banker & Asset Manager

Tutu Agyare has worked in the financial services sector for over 20 years and was the Global Head of Emerging European Equities for UBS Warburg, a division of UBS, a top tier investment banking and securities firm and one of the largest global asset managers.

Born in Kingsbury, London, he relocated with his family to Ghana in 1971 where he completed most of his education. After University, he came back to the UK and joined O'Connor Securities, a boutique trading firm on the floor of the London Stock Exchange in 1986. Tutu made history not only as the first African but as the first black trader on the floor of the London Stock Exchange.

Tutu has held a variety of positions in O'Connor, SBC and now UBS, primarily in a trading role, and was extensively involved with marketing, research and advising major corporations. While at UBS, Tutu ran the UBS Investment Bank's trade in equities in the Euro time-zone Emerging Markets Division, a region that includes Russia and Eastern European countries, Turkey, Israel, the Middle East and all of sub-Saharan Africa, and was a member of the Investment Bank Board.

Tutu is a Managing Partner at Nubuke Investments, an asset management firm focused solely on Africa, which he founded in 2007 and he was the first African appointed as a non-executive Director of Tullow Oil. He has a degree in Mathematics and Computing and is a Director of the Nubuke Foundation in Ghana.

I was educated…

… at Achimota School and the University of Ghana, where I got a BSc Hons degree in Maths and Computing.

My first job was…

… as a floor trader on the London Stock Exchange.

What I do now is…

… run my own asset management company that invests solely in Africa.

What I learned along the way is…

… if anybody has a problem with who you are, let them stress about it; you should not spend any time thinking about it.

My greatest influence has been…

… Kwame Nkrumah, the man who led Ghana to independence from British rule in 1957 and who became the country's first President.

The best advice I ever received is…

… do what you want to do, be what you want to be – and the only limitation is in your mind.

My top tips for succeeding in my career are…

• Don't be afraid to lead and take decisions.

• Don't be afraid to train someone to replace you so that you can look for your next role.

- Don't be afraid to take a stretch position – something that offers a challenge – when it is offered.

- Make sure that every year you learn something new needed for the next rung on the ladder.

- Whilst it is paramount to have goals, make sure you have fun along the way.

Uduak Amimo

Journalist & News Editor

Uduak Amimo chose to become a journalist after becoming frustrated with the images and stories about Africa while in university.

Uduak started her journalism career whilst studying International Relations at the United States International University in Nairobi, where she helped launch the first campus newspaper. Later she would become its Editor. Uduak then went on to work as an Assistant Producer at Reuters Television with Reuters News Agency in Kenya. She then travelled to the US for her Masters degree in Journalism and Public Policy, after which she worked for Voice of America (VOA).

On her return to Kenya, she was recruited by the BBC as a producer and presenter with the English-language BBC African news and current affairs programmes, Network Africa and Focus on Africa. She was then appointed Senior Editorial Adviser, supporting the Director of the BBC World Service, and advised on the editorial leadership and management of the world's leading international radio broadcaster and its New Media operations. Her role also included facilitating editorial collaborations between the World Service and the BBC's international news services.

Uduak strongly believes in the power of education and mentoring to change lives and has been named as one of East Africa's most influential women by an East African magazine.

I was educated...

... all over the place! In Kenya, at Lavington Primary and St George's Primary schools. In between that, a 3-year stint in the US, at Roosevelt Elementary School in Ames, Iowa; in Nigeria, the Navy Primary and Secondary schools, back to Kenya and the Bunyore Girls High School. I went on to do my BA in International Relations at the United States International University in Nairobi, Kenya, graduating with honours. I then won a scholarship and teaching assistantship for an MA in Journalism and Public Policy at the American University in Washington, DC.

My first job was...

... Assistant Producer, Reuters Television in Kenya.

What I do now is...

... that I am the deputy Editor in Chief of an African satellite TV station called NN24. In this role, I am responsible for the news and content that goes out on air. I am also responsible for the journalists.

What I learned along the way is...

... lots of things.

- Believe in, respect and value yourself, surround yourself with people who believe in you, value you and bring out the best in you.

- Be a constructive and positive influence on others.

- Know yourself and your values and what motivates you. If you don't know yourself, you're open to aimlessly wandering through life and being manipulated

- Follow your heart – have a dream, purpose and a vision and pursue them relentlessly!

- Have and keep your faith!

- Always make time to be alone with yourself, clearing your mind and spirit of the clutter we imbibe daily

- Give something back; to your family, community, country etc.

My greatest influence has been…

… a number of people but my late Uncle, Professor Reuben J Olembo tops the list. He believed in me, valued me and brought out the best in me. A few of my university professors who pushed and prodded me, like Dr Cathy Powell and Professor Korwa Adar, and wouldn't let me rest on my laurels.

The best advice I ever received is…

… 'When one door is closed, another is opened.' It's not always obvious, though, when your gaze is fixed on the door that's just slammed in your face! From the Bible, 'All things come together for the good of them that love the Lord'.

My top tips for succeeding in my career are…

- Passion: I really wanted and still want to make a difference in the lives of Africans and people of African descent.

- Knowing your strengths and weaknesses. I have always done psychometric tests to understand myself, my talents and my passions better. For instance, communication and expression are my strengths and impatience is one of my weaknesses. So I know what works for me and what doesn't. Knowing and understanding me helps to understand other people.

- Having a networking/mentoring attitude. I started out thinking that my work could and should speak for itself and that would be it. It hasn't. People have opened doors for me, stood up for me and helped my progress because as I grew older, I learned the lesson that I had to reach out, be help-able and, in turn, help others.

- Knowing what you want. I knew I wanted to be a journalist, so I became one. I knew I wanted to work for Reuters, so I did. I knew I wanted to work for the BBC and I have and I knew I wanted to move back to Africa, and I have. Once you are clear in your mind about what you want, things usually start to fall into place. It's also easier for people to help you when they know what it is you want.

Farouk Haruna

Financial Consultant

Farouk Haruna has built a long career in finance. He started his career in Accounting, crunching inventory and currency accounts for three years for a marine company in Surrey.

He then moved into personal financial management some 11 years ago where his role has varied from tied agent to adviser and finally as a Consultant. He currently works with Ablestoke Consulting in the City of London.

Farouk is also the Membership and Business Development Coordinator for Star 100, a Ghanaian professional network with over 500 members in London.

With what little free time he has, Farouk dedicates his knowledge and experience to charitable organisations. Over the years he has worked with and sat on the boards of both local and international charities with varying objectives ranging from child welfare, women's rights and adult literacy to neighborhood network development, to name a few.

I was educated at...

... the University of London and the Financial Training Company

My first job was...

... an Inventory accountant for European Marine Contractors.

What I do now is...

... work as a Financial Consultant, helping individuals to make the most of their money by giving market advice on investments, retirement planning, mortgages and insurance. The recent introduction of RDR and Pension Compulsion has seen my business move more towards the corporate client.

What I learned along the way is...

... it is not "timing the market" but "time in the market" that makes all the difference.

My greatest influence has been...

... my mother, who constantly drove home the importance of morals and values.

The best advice I ever received is...

... from my parents. The only person who will pay you what you're really worth is yourself, so be your own boss.

My top tips for succeeding in my career are....

*   You can never know enough; the more courses you go on and stay abreast of changes in legislation, the better you get at the job.

- Don't let anyone tell you '*you* can't do it'. If it can be done, it can be done by you.

- There will be peaks as well as troughs; the secret is to have enough peaks so that the troughs don't matter.

- Make sure you enjoy what you do.

Helen Van De Kaa

Public Relations & Marketing Director

Helen Van De Kaa was born in Nigeria and was raised and educated in London. With her strong educational background and degree in Music and Media Management, Helen has been able to use the experiences she has gained from working for various organisations and companies around the UK to develop and manage strong relationships with various people within the music and media world.

Helen's experience includes working at American Express in the exclusive Centurion Department in 2002, getting her first break into the world of public relations, before working for the UK's leading magazine publisher IPC Media in 2004.

Today, Helen is joint Chief Executive Officer of ViVi Cosmetics UK, a family owned business founded in 1992 by her mother-in-law, and which Helen now runs with her husband Jan Hendrik Van De Kaa.

ViVi is a cosmetics brand for all women of colour looking for cosmetics that work for them and does what it says on the label. ViVi Cosmetics have extended their service beyond being a cosmetics brand for ethnic people to finding effective ways to support other organisations, including various charities. By giving effective advice and information; their vision is to make ViVi a lifestyle and not just another cosmetics product.

Helen has always had a passion for beauty and fashion and enjoyed a brief period of modelling in her early years.

In her spare time she plans to create an online magazine for other young women who want to get into the modelling world, giving advice and valuable tips on the trade from former modelling friends. She also plans to publish a book based on her early childhood experiences.

I was educated at…

…. Croydon College and studied for a BTEC National Diploma in Media, followed by a BA degree in Music and Media Management at London Metropolitan.

My first job was…

… miles away from what I wanted – being a waitress at my local restaurant down the road from where I lived! My first more influential job was my intern job working for American Express in the PR department for their Centurion Card and Magazine.

What I do now is…

… I am the joint owner, with my husband, of ViVi Cosmetics UK, which is an online cosmetics website for the Afro Cosmopolitan woman of today.

What I learned along the way is…

… that if you believe in something enough, you can reach all limits and overcome barriers and that nothing is too great for God to do. Most importantly, that you need to believe in yourself and what you can do, and never leave it to others.

My greatest influence has been…

… 3 main factors. One being God – with him all things are possible; second, my mother, who has always encouraged me to work hard to see the benefits unfold; and, finally, my husband, who is my backbone in everything I do. Amongst everything else, he has always believed in me and encouraged me to know that there is nothing I can't do and that, if I want it, I should take it with both hands.

The best advice I ever received was...

... to always learn from your mistakes and adapt to your surroundings. You may fall at the first hurdle but the real difference is whether you can get up again and overcome those barriers and excel. I like to remember the fact that 'I am a Conqueror'.

My top tips for succeeding in my career are...

- Believe in yourself; believe in YOU and what you are trying to achieve.

- Visualise what you want from your career and never be afraid to go out and do it on your own. It takes strength and courage to really follow through with your dreams.

- Always remember that success does not happen overnight and be prepared to struggle for a year or two. You will overcome difficulties and you will be successful.

- If you don't believe in what you are trying to achieve or do in your career, you can't expect anyone else to.

Ade Daramy

Writer, Broadcaster & Press Officer

Adeyemi Olusegun Abiose Daramy is a Sierra Leonean (despite those Nigerian forenames), who attended school in Sierra Leone and the UK. I am a journalist and broadcaster with over 20 years' experience, broadcasting and writing on mainly, but not exclusively, African affairs for a number of publications including the much-missed *West Africa* magazine and The Guardian. I have written on politics in Sierra Leone, Ivory Coast, Guinea, Gambia, Nigeria and for two years edited the UK government's Cabinet Office's magazine *Modernising Government Now.* From 1997-2007, I edited *Mano Vision,* an African affairs magazine.

I am a founder-member of the Sierra Leone Diaspora Network, which encourages the Diaspora to invest and eventually return to assist in the rebuilding of our country. I also work with several schools in Sierra Leone and use my network to bring them equipment and improved facilities.

I am a former Senior Policy Advisor to the UK Cabinet Office, advising on data protection and Freedom of Information laws. I currently work as a Press and Communications Officer for the Insolvency Service, a UK government Executive Agency. I'm fanatical about music (all types) and sports (most, but especially football – Man United fan from birth – it's a long story!).

I intend to return home in the very near future as I believe that what little I can offer is more needed there than here. I am a firm believer in Black organizations working together to uplift our whole community, wherever they may be.

I was educated at…

… Sierra Leone Grammar School and Christ the King College, Bo, Sierra Leone, followed by the then-North London Polytechnic (UK).

My first job was…

… in a William Hill betting shop as a 'board man'.

What I do now is…

… Press Officer and Communications for a UK government Executive Agency.

What I learned along the way is…

… you learn something new everyday; some useful, some not (or so you might think, until they help you win a general knowledge quiz!).

My greatest influence has been…

… words of wisdom and encouragement from my parents.

The best advice I ever received was…

… "No two people are alike, so be yourself always; don't try and be anyone else, not even Pelé!"

My top tips for succeeding in my career are…

- It may seem obvious, but pursue a career that you either have a liking or the skills for. If you go with former, but not the latter, you can always learn or study to get skills. Nothing can teach you to like a career that you start out hating.

- Don't be pressured into doing something just because 'it's the family tradition'. If you'd rather be a footballer than a surgeon and you have the aptitude for the one and not the other, try and bring friends and family around to your point of view. It's your life; no one can live it for you. The same applies to a career.

- Set yourself high standards. If you are doing a piece of work, ask yourself whether you would be happy if you were the recipient. Never fall into the temptation of leaving a job half-done just because you are tired. Be your own harshest critic. If you start out like that, you'll find you can cope with anyone else's criticism.

- Pace yourself: not everyone can perform brilliant last-minute miracles in delivering work. Make sure that you give yourself time to look back and review your work before you present it.

- You'll never be too old to learn and you'll learn something valuable and new every day. You can learn from those both older and younger than you. The young have the vitality of discovering and exploring all that is new and exciting. The old have the benefit of having 'been there and done that'. Leave yourself open to acquiring knowledge. Read, read, read and read again.

Professor Felix Konotey-Ahulu

Medical Consultant

Professor Felix I D Konotey-Ahulu is the Dr Kwegyir Aggrey Distinguished Professor of Human Genetics at the University of Cape Coast, Ghana and a Consultant Physician/Genetic Counsellor, Haemoglobinopathy/Sickle Cell States, in Harley Street, London.

Born in Ghana, Professor Konotey-Ahulu attended Achimota School and the University College of the Gold Coast, before reading Medicine in London, qualifying MB BS. After a period back in the newly independent Ghana as a Medical Officer, he returned to the UK for his postgraduate studies in Tropical Medicine, earning a Doctorate in Medicine with subsequent postings at the University of Ghana Medical School and the Ministry of Health at Korle Bu Hospital, where he directed the largest Sickle Cell Clinic in the world.

A global authority on the Sickle Cell disease, the value of Professor Konotey-Ahulu's work, which has included discoveries in Clinical Medicine, has been widely recognized by medical practitioners and specialists around the world, leading to his inclusion in a survey of 'The 100 Greatest Africans of All Time'. He has produced upwards of 200 publications, a number of which have become the definitive studies in their field.

Professor Konotey-Ahulu is the first person known to have traced hereditary disease in his forebears, generation by generation, with all the names, right back to 1670 AD. http://www.konotery-ahulu.com/images/generation.jpg.

He is the recipient of numerous awards including the Dr. Martin Luther King Jr. Foundation Award for outstanding research in Sickle Cell Anaemia, the Guinness Award for Scientific Achievement in the Commonwealth, and the Gold Medal of Ghana's Academy of Arts & Sciences for outstanding contribution to knowledge in the Medical Sciences by a Ghanaian.

I was educated at...

... Presbyterian/Basel Mission Schools in the Gold Coast (Ghana), before I completed my Cambridge School Certificate & London Matriculation in Achimota School. I graduated from London University's Westminster Hospital School of Medicine. Later, I attended Liverpool University for a Diploma in Tropical Medicine, and then Cambridge University, Christ's College, where I was a Schofield Fellow.

My first job was...

... as a doctor – a 'House Physician' in a London Hospital.

What I do now is...

... practise as a Consultant Physician and Genetic Counsellor, advising people on how to find out the chances of hereditary disease like Sickle Cell Disease (the AcheAche Syndrome) in their offspring. I conduct the Annual Kwegyir Aggrey Prize Examination at the University of Cape Coast in Ghana. Teaching and answering queries from around the world through my website occupies much of my time, day and night.

What I learned along the way is...

... that 'The Fear of GOD is The Beginning of Wisdom'.

My greatest influence has been...

... Papaa and Mamma, Rev and Mrs D A Konotey-Ahulu.

The best advice I ever received is...

... Longfellow's poem that Papaa taught me when I was 9:

> "The heights by great men reached and kept
> Were not attained by sudden flight;
> But they, while their companions slept,
> Kept toiling upward in the night".

My top tips for succeeding in my career are...

- Fear God and love God in equal measures (First Book of Corinthians Chapter 2 verse 9, and Romans Chapter 8 verse 32).

- Cultivate how to think, not just what to think. Textbooks, teachers, radio, television, internet, newspapers, magazines already tell us constantly what to think, which is not always enough for success. To achieve great things, learn how to think.

- Choose friends that will not lead you astray.

- Learn to be able to say 'NO!' when everyone else is saying 'YES, please".

Toyin Dania

Business Counsellor

Toyin Dania is Manager of Business Counselling and Training Services at Wandsworth Youth Enterprise Centre (WYEC).

Born in South London and educated in Nigeria, Sussex and Essex, Toyin is the second of 14 children. Her role includes managing the day to day running of the Counselling department, providing one-to-one Business Counselling at pre-start and post-start up stages and encouraging motivation and self empowerment from the initial stages to setting up a business. WYEC's support continues for 2 years and is backed up by Business training, including Marketing and Finance.

She oversees the low-cost business start-up units and the Business Incubation side of the programme, organising and participating in the training sessions and Business Awareness seminars and other marketing activity. Toyin also oversees strategic business development nationally and internationally, alongside the Senior Management Team.

For two years, Toyin has also run her own Consultancy – TD Consultants Ltd – which supports entrepreneurs with Mentoring and Coaching. She continues to develop herself with training in partnership with Success University – a life-long learning company. Toyin volunteers her time with a charity (African Foundation For Development (AFFORD)) which sets up projects like Supporting Entrepreneurs and Enterprise Development in Africa (SEEDA) and helps to develop strategies to build sustainable business support and an "each one teach one attitude".

Toyin lives in Essex and loves personal development, quality time with friends and family, salsa, skiing and travelling.

I was educated at...

... Basildon College (BTEC National Diploma in Business and Finance), followed by City University (Diploma in Counselling) and Newcastle College (Life Coaching – Certificate and Diploma) and SFEDI, where I completed the Accredited Business Counsellor Programme.

My first job was...

... Senior Training Consultant at Sight and Sound Education Ltd, where I supported young people and women back to work by developing and training them in business skills.

What I do now is...

... manage the Business Counselling and Training Services at Wandsworth Youth Enterprise Centre (WYEC). I have worked for the last eight years with my team of Business Counsellors and Outreach workers who provide and develop entrepreneurship programmes for young people aged 14-30 on self-employment awareness, personal development, business training and support.

What I learned along the way is...

• Have passion for your work.

• Work from a position of integrity.

• Give more than you receive.

• Work with everyone – we all have something to learn or share.

• Remember that your reputation is all you have.

• Have fun and balance your time with work and pleasure.

My greatest influence has been…

… Nelson Mandela and my Aunty Fashola.

The best advice I ever received is…

- Don't give up.

- You get out of life what you put in, so help out when and where you can.

- It is never too late.

- Ask and it shall be given.

My top tips for my career are…

- Be curious – find out about everything, you never know when you might need that gem of information.

- Be persistent – you never know how far away you are from you aspirations if you do not keep going.….you will find out sooner than you think.

- Be ambitious – how else can you be? There are always going to be more challenges; just plan to always meet them and you will feel more alive for doing so.

- Be compassionate – there are always people who can do and always those who cannot do. Give a helping hand once in a while and also take one yourself.

- Remain up to date with the world and the people around you.

- Be focused but make time to play and relax; that means laughing too.

Kwamina Monney

Architect

Kwamina Monney's interest in craft, colour and the hand-drawn mark derives from a Ghanaian heritage and time spent working in Malaysia exploring the relationship between nature and technology. He has an honours degree from the Hull School of Architecture where he was nominated for the RIBA President's Bronze Medal and a double postgraduate degree with distinction in Architecture from Oxford Brookes University. Kwamina attained the RIBA Part III qualification from Kingston University.

Kwamina is a former Director at AL_A, where he led, amongst others, the team redeveloping the 1.0 million sq ft media campus for News Corporation, the refurbishment of Conde Nast's executive floors in London, re-modeling the Rinascente department store in Milan and the complex master planning and redevelopment of the Globe Academy for ARK. His previous offices include Ian Simpson Architects, Lifschutz Davidson Sandilands, Horden Cherry Lee Architects and Ngiom Partnership, Kuala Lumpur Malaysia.

Kwamina has been published in the BD Class of 2000, has been a visiting critic at universities in the UK, a jury panelist for Blueprint & WAN awards and is a published illustrator.

I was educated at...

RIBA Pt1 Hull School of Architecture, UK

RIBA Pt2 Oxford Brookes University, UK

RIBA Pt3 University of Kingston-upon-Thames, UK

My first job was...

... in Kuala Lumpur, Malaysia, on completing the Pt1 course.

What I do now is...

... work as an architect and, as seamlessly as possible, work collaboratively with clients and specialists to conceive, design and deliver original architecture, interior spaces or objects that respond to a complex set of criteria, but are always rooted and contextualised to their environment or function.

What I learned along the way is...

... the need to have a particular interest whilst maintaining a broad knowledge base and practical ability; to set new challenges and test perceptions of established boundaries; to continually evolve and look to the future whilst respecting the legacies and achievements of history – the past can present the future. Also to maintain a self-propelling, dynamic motivation and self belief, with a reasonable dose of reality!

My greatest influence has been...

... the desire to set the benchmark

The best advice I ever received is...

... being reminded that the glass is always half full.

My top tips for succeeding in my career area are...

- Be flexible, keeping an open mind and being adaptable to change.

- Innovate, be proactive, seek out knowledge.

- Diplomacy and measure – at the right time and place, say what needs to be said, having first considered all of the options.

- Clairvoyance – acquire through experience the ability to forsee a problem or opportunity and react ahead of time.

- The best type of problem solving comes through lateral or divergent thinking.

- Scale – seeing 'the wood from the trees' with the ability to operate in varying contexts and points in a process simultaneously.

- Be part of the team – a collaborative mindset is central to a successful outcome.

- Learn to worry less about others and more about yourself.

- Maintain your composure. Don't panic, remain mentally and physically calm at all times.

- Relax – take time to recharge!

Marjorie Ngwenya

Actuary

Marjorie Ngwenya is the Editor of The Actuary, the magazine of the UK actuarial profession.

A qualified actuary (Fellow of the Institute of Actuaries), who specialises in risk management, Marjorie gained her actuarial qualification at Deloitte where she held roles in the UK, Netherlands and Canada.

Marjorie has previously held the positions of Business Development Manager at GenRe and Senior Risk Actuary at Swiss Re.

She is currently the Head of Governance and Risk Management at Acorn Fund Management. Marjorie's experience spans the fields of pensions, fund management, life insurance and health insurance.

Marjorie serves on the Board of Trustees for the Legal Assistance Trust supporting the Legal Resources Centre of South Africa.

I was educated at…

… Midlands Christian College and Chisipite Senior School, both in Zimbabwe, and the London School of Economics.

My first job was…

… working as a croupier during university.

What I do now is…

… I am a Risk Manager for a fund management firm and Editor of The Actuary magazine.

What I learned along the way is…

… little that is worthwhile in life is effortless.

My greatest influence has been…

… my parents and inspiring career role models I've met along the way.

The best advice I ever received was…

… your life is 10% what happens to you and 90% how you react to it.

My top tips for succeeding in my career area are…

- Always being willing to learn.

- Approaching my work and career with enthusiasm.

- Not seeing my race and gender as disadvantages, but rather as differentiating factors.

Everyday Heroes

Projects and Exercises

Now that you have read **Everyday Heroes**, here are some projects and exercises that you can do, either in school or at home.

These projects and exercises will:

- Help you improve your writing skills and give you practice in asking questions and listening to others;

- Give you some ideas on how to find out more about careers that interest you;

- Offer you tips on how to think about your own skills and the kind of jobs that match your skills;

- Help you learn more from the careers of the people interviewed in **Everyday Heroes**; and

- Show you how to find out what you are good at and what you should do next.

Project 1 – Interview Your Own Everyday Heroes

Choose up to 3 people and interview them to find out about their lives and careers. These can be family members, teachers, family friends or people within your community.

Use the following questions to structure your interview.

Name:

Occupation:

1. I was educated at…

2. My first job was…

3. What I do now is…

4. What I learned along the way is…

5. My greatest influence has been…

6. The best advice I ever received is…

7. My top tips for succeeding in my career area are…

Write a biography of the person

Include information about:

- Where they were born and grew up.

- The kind of courses and subjects they studied.

- The kinds of jobs they have done.

- Any awards or prizes they have received.

- Anything that you think makes them special and a good role model for other people.

- **Include a photograph of the person.**

Always remember to first get permission from the people you interview to share their story with your class or group.

Project 2 – Research a Career of your Choice

From the interviews in the book, choose a career that you think sounds interesting and find out more about it.

To help you with your research:

- Look for books in your school library or local library that can tell you more about this career.

- Use the internet to help you find out more about this career.

- Ask a Careers Advisor for more information about this career.

- Research the kind of subjects or courses that you would need to take to be able to do this career well.

- Think about the kind of skills that would be needed for this career.

- Explain why you think this would be an interesting career choice for you.

Exercise 1 – Thinking About My Future Career

Thinking about which career to choose can seem daunting at first. There seem to be a huge number of things that you could do with your life and at this stage it may not be crystal clear to you what type of work would give you satisfaction and enjoyment.

Reading about the different people in **Everyday Heroes** will have:-

- Given you some idea of the types of jobs and careers that might interest you.

- Given you an idea of how people have broken into a particular career.

- Sparked your interest further as to how you might investigate what a particular job or career entails.

- Shown you what it is possible to achieve – given some hard work!

Different Jobs Need Different Skills

One way of thinking about the type of work that will interest you is to break a job down into different *skills*. A skill may be something that you can actually do, like being able to put together flat pack furniture from a set of instructions, or write a computer program or paint a picture. Or it may be something which is less visible, like being good at supporting someone when they are going through a tough time, or building friendships easily with others or being able to come up with really interesting ideas.

One way of grouping these skills is to divide them into skills to do with **People**, **Data**, **Ideas** and **Things**.

People skills are about relating to others. So it might be about how you build a relationship with someone, how you put them at their ease, how you negotiate with them or lead a group of people to do something. So a sports team captain whose job is to motivate his or her team to do well would be expected to have fairly strong people skills.

Data skills are about working with information. So these skills are about being able to collect data, understand and manipulate figures, analyse them and come up with a story and conclusion about what it all means. A researcher who wanted to know how much money different groups of people spend on going to the cinema, and what types of films they see would be expected to have strong data skills.

Ideas skills are about being creative. These skills are about coming up with ideas, solving problems, creating things from scratch, but will include being able to communicate these ideas well to other people. So a team who designs a new type of smart phone which is radically different from every type of mobile that has gone before would be expected to have strong ideas skills.

Things skills are about making things. They are about building things, putting them together, and possibly manufacturing them from raw materials. So a couple who decide to build their own home and do the majority of it themselves would be expected to have strong things skills

You may have already spotted that most jobs will require a mix of these different types of skills.

In the example of the researcher above, he or she may use predominately data skills, but would require ideas skills to come up with a questionnaire that is clearly written and attractive to fill in. If they were stopping people as they went into the cinema to answer the questionnaire face to face, they might also require people skills to persuade people to give up five minutes of their time.

Skills and Values

1. **Can you give an example from your own life at school, home or elsewhere where you have used a skill from each of these categories?**

2. **Would you say you have stronger People, Data, Ideas or Things Skills?**

3. **For which category did you found it hardest to come up with an example?**

Choose 5 profiles from *Everyday Heroes* and then answer these questions:-

1. **For this person, would you imagine they had stronger People, Data, Ideas or Things Skills?**

2. **What makes you say that?**

3. **On a scale of 1 to 10, where 1 is "I couldn't see myself doing this job in a million years" and 10 is "I'd really like to tell people that this is what I do for a living", where would you place yourself against each job?**

In addition to skills, there are lots of other influences that may encourage someone to take a particular career path, including:

*   Their values – wanting to improve the world, show integrity, act honestly.

*   The influence of people they looked up to when they were growing up, or as adults.

*   The kind of education that they had.

As you are reading through the 5 profiles you have chosen, make a note if you think that there was a very strong influence from one of these categories.

You can create a grid like this and fill it out as you read through to collate your answers:-

Name of Person Being Interviewed	What do they do?	Strongest Skill P, D, I or T for People, Data, Ideas, Things	Can I see myself doing this? (1-10) 1 = No way! 10 = Yes!	Other strong influences

Now you have filled out your grid, pick the three that have the highest "Can I see myself doing this?" scores and answer these questions:-

1.   Is there any common thread between the three people that you have chosen?

2.   What is it about these careers that makes you curious about them?

3.   Are the strongest skills for these three people the same or different?

4.   Are you strongly influenced by values that you hold, people that you look up to or the education that you have received?

Exercise 2 – Finding out What I am Good At

From the previous exercise, you may now have an idea as to what kind of skills you are strongest in. There are some skills, such as being good at Maths, that you may use a lot at school and not so much in the outside world. Others, such as People skills, you may use all the time with friends, family and organisations such as churches or clubs.

For this exercise, think about the things that you enjoy doing or helping with. You may not have redecorated a room or serviced an engine, but you may be interested in it through the people around you.

You will see overleaf some examples of the different types of skills in the different categories.

Circle the ones that you enjoy – or think you would enjoy doing – and then add other examples from your own experiences in the blank spaces below them. At the end put a number which is number of items you have circled <u>plus</u> the number of items you have added.

People	Data	Ideas	Things
Listen to a friend's problems	Find out facts and figures for an area you are interested in – a sports team?	Design things	Make things in Woodwork, Metalwork or assemble models
Teach others how to do something	Perform scientific experiments	Write stories	Sew, knit, make crafts
Lead a team	Write computer programmes	Draw and paint	Work in the garden
Persuade someone to buy something	Solve logic puzzles	Decorate a room	Cooking and baking
Total Circled:	**Total Circled:**	**Total Circled:**	**Total Circled:**
1			
2			
3			
4			
5			
6			
7			
8			
9			
10			
Total Added:	**Total Added:**	**Total Added:**	**Total Added:**
Overall People:	**Overall Data:**	**Overall Ideas:**	**Overall Things:**

My top score is   ....   and is for   ....   skills

My 2nd score is   ....   and is for   ....   skills

My 3rd score is   ....   and is for   ....   skills

My lowest score is   ....   and is for   ....   skills

Did this match what you said in the previous exercise that you thought would be your strongest skill area, or is it different?

In what way is it different?

Use your answer to find out about more jobs that would require the strongest skill area you have identified.

Exercise 3 – What Should I do Next?

If you are not sure which career would suit you, remember that a career isn't always something that people decide on when they are young and then do for the rest of their lives.

Today, people have more choices about what they want to do and at which times in their lives that they want to do them.

When you first start a career, some things like earning a good salary or building a great reputation or finding something where you are continually learning, may be very important to you. Later on in your life, different things often take over and, for some people, it may become more important to find a job with stability or just doing something that you really love.

My Type of Career

The skills exercises that you have completed so far should give you some clues about the type of careers that you can investigate further. But there are lots of other things to take into account.

For example, if you are a really hands-on, practical person who learns best by doing something, then choosing a career where you need to do a lot of reading and learning from books, like lawyers do, is going to present you with some difficulties.

Equally, if you like working in a fun and busy environment where you don't know what is happening from one day to the next, then a job that is very routine, repetitious and full of rules and regulations will not be of interest to you.

To help you find a starting point for you to investigate more about a particular career, fill in the following:-

The three people interviewed in *Everyday Heroes* that I found most interesting and inspiring were:-

1. .... who did ....

2. .... who did ....

3. .... who did ....

My strongest to weakest group of skills are:-

1.

2.

3.

4.

My three favourite subjects at School are/were:-

1.

2.

3.

I tend to learn best when…

I would like to find out more about a career as…

.

My starting point for this is…

Happy investigating!

About the Author

Frances Mensah Williams is a writer, coach and Human Resources consultant with over twenty years experience of developing and managing people.

Her experience covers a diverse range of sectors including international development, advertising, media, banking and financial services. She has worked at senior levels for leading private sector companies as well as with public sector organisations in Europe and Africa.

Winner of awards including the BFIIN 2005 Gold Award for Innovative Capacity Building, the GPA 2005 Innovative Business Award and the 2005 Black Enterprise Rising Star Award, she is passionately interested in working with people, particularly those facing career and cultural change, to develop their potential.

Frances has worked for many years as a career coach, assisting senior executives, business school graduates and young people to identify and implement their career progression strategies. Frances delivers training seminars and careers workshops to a wide range of people and with her experience and understanding of both emerged and emerging markets, she is able to bring a unique insight into the challenges faced by professionals working in today's globalised marketplace.

Frances is also the founder and Editor of ReConnect Africa (www.reconnectafrica.com) an award-winning online careers, news and business publication and portal for professionals of Africa heritage. She is active in speaking engagements and in writing on issues relating to skills development in Africa and harnessing the talents of the African Diaspora. She sits on and chairs a number of committees and working groups.

In 2011, Frances was named as one of the *Top 20 Inspirational Females from the Africa Diaspora in Europe* by ADIPWE (African Diaspora Professional Women in Europe).

Frances is married with two children.